The Beauty of Silence

– ASHOK SAWHNY –

An environmentally friendly book printed and bound in England by
www.printondemand-worldwide.com

This book is made entirely of chain-of-custody materials

www.fast-print.net/store.php

THE BEAUTY OF SILENCE

A catalogue record for this book is available from the British Library

ISBN 978-178456-093-5

First published 2014 by
FASTPRINT PUBLISHING
Peterborough, England.

Contents

1.

The Beauty of Silence

The unspeaking hills,
The whispers from the streams,
The beating of my heart,
The quietude of the stars
That just light my way,
Clouds in the sky that do gently sway,
What greater beauty will I ever find,
Than the beauty of silence
And the untroubled mind.

How serene I am when with myself,
No words do I need to converse
With the one I know best of all,
The only one I know, perhaps, at all.

The heart and the mind and I all one,
Silence the medium that unites me with
Me, and with all things else,
And silence that sets me free.

For I am my own best friend
My confidant,
The one from whom nothing is veiled,
Conscience asleep, until aroused by
Silence.

The fabric of silence is a golden weave,
Awe and majesty its sceptre and crown,
Why would I want to be in the rabble,
And silence unhappily drown?

A silent moment with one's self,
Worth more than a million hours of power and pelf.

2.
The Cloven Hoof

Show me not the cloven hoof,
For the nature of man I know,
Part descendant of the fallen angel,
Those traits does he often show.

Ancestry does a role play
In the makings of one and all,
A strange amalgam is Man, for sure,
Whom do I good or bad, call.

A metaphor for angel and monster both,
Or saint and sinner if you wish,
The holy and unholy all,
A strangely made-up dish.

Think, and I think you'll agree with me,
And eye to eye with me see,
Zephyr and storm all in one,
When all is simply said and done.

3.
I Remember

The freshness of dew, the verdant scene,
All around me the beauty of green,
The colour green makes Nature supreme,
And makes everything look like a beautiful dream.
I Remember.

Memory is but a mistress fickle,
The pebbles I played with in the stream,
'Twas up in the mountains of Kashmir,
Where dawn and the sun were awe extreme.
I Remember.

The ripples now a faint memory,
I remember the taste of strawberry and cream,
What good the wisdom that comes with age,
The magic of childhood an unbeatable dream.
I Remember.

Re-live I do those memories old,
Where the end of anything is never in sight,
Where elves and goblins and the like,
Never turned demons in the middle of night.
I Remember.

Inhibition a word foreign to the tongue,
The bells of fear just never rung,
Mum and dad always around,
Their gentle footsteps, the most soothing sound.
I Remember.

Nostalgia is both kind and unkind,
But the innocence of childhood is divine,
For God rests in the heart of the child,
And these words, Ashok, are everyone's and mine.

4.

Hope And Prayer - A Potent Mix

Hope and prayer are the potent mix
That help you realize,
Some dreams, some desires too,
And quieten unrelenting sighs.

Life is like the ocean
Whose waves you cannot quell,
But ride them you can and triumphantly,
When you keep them under your spell.

And for that you need what the first verse said,
Cos faith moves mountains we know,
The ocean knows and all too well,
Storms are transient, they come and go.

Prayers have wings did you know,
With angels as their carriers?
For they know best where God lives,
And thus face no mortal barriers.

The mind at rest is the one with hope
And an honest prayer on the lips,
So keep these two always alive
And on your fingertips.

5.

My Little Corner

I love my little corner,
Where sequestered I can be,
Solace is the balm I seek,
And a chance to be with me.

It's beautiful, my little corner,
Tucked away somewhere,
Where only I can access it,
Cos only I for it care.

If you want to know where it is,
You'd have to look inside, of you,
And strange as this may sound,
It is, indubitably, true.

For all such corners lie,
Within the pulsating heart,
Where journeys all will one day end,
And from where they all start.

And that's where my little corner is,
To which I often retire,
Sometimes for some moments of peace,
And sometimes for the day entire.

6.

To My Children

May your river of love never run dry,
May blue be the permanent colour of your sky,
May tears never wet your smiling eyes,
May smiles be yours, no cause for sighs.

May all your hopes and wishes too
Listen to you and then come true,
May no journey ever be too long,
May you always be singing a happy song.

May you be blessed to know and understand,
The difference between right and wrong,
May your nights and days never heavy be,
And burdens light, as light can be.

May you never think or do another harm,
And yourself be blessed with eternal calm,
May storms in your life quickly subside,
May smooth and peaceful be your life's ride.

Can't wish you more, my dear children,
My good wishes always by your side.

7.
Not So Poor Is Poor Old Poetry

Destined to never a victor be,
Poetry is the victim of destiny,
How unmusical is the world today,
Only prose used, to say what we say.
Fiction is what truly sells,
Telling stories rings the bells,
So humdrum is the state of life,
Dreams are sold and merchants rife.
And yet verses quoted everywhere,
From parliament to the fair out there,
Common and uncommon folks,
Keats quote and Shakespeare revere.
Ghalib in another world,
Encomiums on Mir unfurled,
Whoever does du Maurier quote,
Agatha all the mystery wrote,
Yet no one does the Christie quote,
Rushdie never saw the light of day,
Whatever he said night had to say,
Hosseini just had suns on the mind,
Cos beautiful stars he just couldn't find.

And who saw skylarks and nightingales,
And who but Homer a ship's sails,
And who but never of Keats heard,
Or swoon did not on a Wordsworth word?

Why then is the poet despondent so,
Why then does he have to publishers go
With folded hands to them entreat,
To be given more than just a tweet?

But don't get me wrong, dear reader,
The poet is no beggar nor pleader,
For he does but from the heart speak,
While the story-teller's a story freak,

So keep your verses always flowing,
Who knows where who is going?
The road to verse may well be the last,
But your words, O poet, will in stone be cast.

8.

The Cycle Of Life

Green to yellow is the cycle of life,
Accept the cycle to live without strife,
Look at trees that wither and droop,
Then backs that are bent and perforce stoop,
Hair once black, silver turns,
Bald the head, don't talk sideburns,
The glint in the eye now a deadpan face,
Snails too quick for any kind of race,
The swagger in the gait, now two left feet,
The look in the mirror the smile doesn't greet,
Lifting the cup a formidable task,
The list of woes too long, don't ask,
The night no longer comfort and rest,
Lying in bed in itself a test,
Cos half the night you wait for the sun,
And the half that's left is spent on the run,
A tussle between the bed and the loo,
Tell me, dear reader, isn't that true?
But don't you now feel sorry for me?
No feelings please of hidden glee,
For I know in the depths of the sordid heart,
I can see waiting darts of hidden envy,
For the contentment that in me you see!!!
Please laugh with me if you will,
Let's do that together at least until,
One of us kicks the proverbial pail,
And one is still left with wind in the sail,
And that one, I hope, is poor little me,
Cos I wouldn't like you to suffer, you see.
HA HA!!

9.

Nothingness

When it's as quiet as it is now,
No sounds but the beat of the heart,
No past, no present, no future,
No gathering and no falling apart,

No broken bits to gather,
No shattered pieces of glass,
No mending, darning, no putting together,
Solitude is a master class,

A nothingness does the air pervade,
And Time its relevance loses,
The mind too, in like, responds,
And quietude wisely chooses,

And Nature too colludes well,
To peace and quiet maintain,
No rustling leaves no warbling birds,
As a state of nothingness, I attain.

The skies and beyond seem nothing too,
Just floating, drifting, silent birds,
An all–encompassing nothingness,
That imprisons my very words.

Nothing is greater than nothingness,
For that is what is happiness.

10.
Grandfather

Austere and simple like a tree,
Standing upright all the while,
No wayward winds could make him bend,
Nor from his face take off the smile.

He was the joker of the pack,
The king of hearts said some,
Others the clown that wore the crown,
For he constantly chewed gum.

The village was small but colourful
And the queen they said was pretty,
The joker though no village fool,
Was the ruler but not so witty.

For wit is not what is needed,
When sincerity is the ask,
And that he had in plenty,
For he never wore a mask.

He had no airs about him,
Nor did he illusions carry,
Straightforward his demeanour,
No cut, no thrust, no parry.

His kingdom was his heart,
His subjects resided there,
He loved them all deeply,
And deeply did he care.

He's the one we call grandfather,
The one who's seen it all,
The one who's there but always,
To help you when you fall.

11.
A Gleam Of Hope

Why does it seem so dark sometimes,
With not a gleam of hope,
Not a sliver of a silver lining do I see,
Cloud with cloud so intertwined
The ray of the sun downcast,
Melancholy,
Unable to cope
With the gloom that surrounds!

Is this all what light is about!
To darkness remove,
Or,
Is there a higher purpose;
To wisdom dispense
And in so doing lighten the grey spirit
To blithely accept,
The darkness.

And in the clouds envision the sun,
That will rise and set too,
And as with seasons all,
Winter, spring, summer, fall,
Accept.

Does not Hope on its loss depend,
As life does on the inevitable end,
Would there be a white without a black,
Or a day without a night?
If black is what hope is not,
Then dawn must bring in the light,

If there was no dark, O poet, think,
There'd be no sleep,
Then how, pray tell me,
How would you with it your tryst keep?

Hope springs eternal in the human breast,
Not my words I know,
Hope it is that keeps at bay
The despondent heart,
And Life aglow.

12.

Go Have A Blast

Couldn't care less for poetry.
And the same goes for philosophy,
Just want to live with fun and joy,
And, somehow, eternally.

What is the point of it all, tell me,
Is life punishment for all who be,
Must we always for mercy beg,
And pray from life to be set free?

Why not then hedonistic become,
Eat and be merry, drink and be numb?
Let the wise spew forth for they will die too.
Why flaunt your nonsense when it's wise to be dumb.

This world's no more than a colourful circus,
Jokers and clowns striving for focus,
Magicians and tricksters are part of life's show,
The circus, after all, is just hocus–pocus.

The one who is cloven between life and death,
Has forgotten the purpose of each vibrant breath,
You can't be living with demise on your mind,
So go have a blast, get out of the bind.

These words are immortal take it from me,
For I've lived it fully, 24 x 7 you see,
And if you still don't get it, my dear friends,
I can only feel for you, and very, very sorry

13.
Non–Believer

The Universe is so big
And my world so small,
I am so tiny
And the trees so tall,

Mountains I climb
And off fountains I fall,
My friend in the sky
I unfailingly call.

And you non-believer
Have the temerity and gall,
To say He's nothing
And you are but all.

What do you do when in despair,
What helps you then
To not stop, stand tall?
When gloom surrounds you
And dark is your pall,
Don't you then waver,
And don't you then stall?
Stumble,
And then also recall,

The stories you heard on granny's knee,
When you were two or maybe three,
Of the God she worshipped,
Framed pictures of prophets
Hanging in the hall.

What made you then what you are now?
O, rational mind,
What an irrational fall!

14.
My Hibiscus

The colour red in my hibiscus
Turns crimson in the cold,
Like glossy, black, hair
That turns silver when old.

Does the flower have a story
Of the life that it lives,
Of the pleasure to the eyes,
And to our senses that it gives?

Smiling in the sun
In the warmth out there,
Looking so very pretty,
With Spring in the air.

The leaves take a leaf
Out of old 'Hibe's' book,
And the two of them together
A dream pair look.

I soak in the beauty
That I see all day,
Knowing fully well
It'll be soon on its way.

For the 'Hibes' short-lived
Just a day and a night,
And its destiny will soon
Extinguish the light.

But alas, that is true
Of all living things,
But I must thank my dear flower,
For the joy that it brings.

So thank you dear 'Hibus'
For I shan't see you tomorrow,
But I'll remember you always
With happiness, not sorrow.

15.
Just Thoughts

The vastness of the sky above,
Is all but out of sight,
For those who are in comfort couched,
Cos the ceiling is their height.

So step out and explore, O folks,
The world that's waiting for you,
With open arms and a welcome warmth,
Pastures green and skies blue.

If a boat you take to nowhere,
Then nowhere will you reach,
Live it full but observe it too,
For life has lessons to teach.

Reach beyond the grasp
Is an adage wise and old,
Timidity will not get you far,
So try being a little bold.

Sermons are but sermons we know,
Poets and preachers the same,
No one reads and no one listens,
Is sermonizing a game?

Holy books are sermons too
Exhorting us to do right,
Not just by the light of day,
But also by the night.

Take heed then,
To what the conscience has to say,
For conscience it is that saves you from
Wayward paths and going astray.

16.
Be Silent As The Mountain

Be silent as the mountain
And meander like the stream,
Go fly to the stars
Go realize your dream.

Dreams take you where
You otherwise don't go,
You'll get to the sea,
If like the river you flow.

And you'll never be a rose
If thorns are your worry,
Let Time make the way,
There's no need to hurry.

The path of the river
Is strewn with rocks,
There's a lesson out there
On how to deal with blocks.

The stillness of the mountain
Is for the wise to perceive,
And from that gentle giant
A lesson to receive.

17.

Now That My Whisky Days Are Over

Now that my whisky days are over,
And no more those rings of smoke,
Life will have a different meaning, I guess,
And different fires will I stoke.

Let's start with introspection,
I'll get to know 'me',
And learn how well I know myself,
Beyond the image I see.

Then shake hands with the past,
And the leaves of history,
Walk down the lanes I once knew well,
And jog a sleeping memory.

Re-live the beauty of childhood,
With the times that have passed me by,
Gaze at the stars in wonder,
And look at the moon and the sky,

Sing me a song, perhaps,
Of melancholy and joy.
Dream of bats and a ball,
Of the times when I was a boy.

I'll never live in the past though,
For that is a battle I'll never win,
Not being in the present mostly,
Is for me an awful sin.

And on that journey, hopefully, find,
The answers to queries that arise,
Of yesteryears and the water that's flown,
Under the bridges and my eyes.

And, on a lighter note, dear reader,
I hope when I do hit the sack,
I hope 'twill be fairies not nightmares,
Or to my whisky I'll be soon back.

18.
Beneath The Skies With The Blue Above

Beneath the skies with the blue above
The mind is a vast open space,
So why would you not the outdoors prefer,
To the traumas on the inside, you face.

No kings, no queens, no castles too,
No greater majesty will you ever see,
Than the warmth and shade that you generously get,
From the beautiful flowering, towering tree.

Incomparable, the vast expanse of desert,
Seen through the eyes of the dromedary,
Incomparable, reds, yellows and oranges,
Of the sun that sets for others to see.

And nothing, but nothing, will ever beat,
The freshness of spring, its scent in the air,
What grandeur then does lie inside,
That keeps you from going out anywhere.

Rivers of joy are better than gloom,
So go step out and joy you'll find,
See how much good the outdoors do,
To a battered, worn-out, thirsting mind.

19.

Know Thyself

Let the eyes of another
Tell you who you are,
And you might then simply find
From yourself, you're very far.

Mirrors may be warped
And reflections not always true,
When you try to fool the mirror
It might well do that to you.

But the eyes of another
Can see through façade,
And games that you play
Are no more than charade.

You can also ask another
Your friend who knows you best,
No one knows you better
Put your Conscience to the test.

With harmony 'tween you and your intrinsic other,
You'll lord over strife and differences smother.

20.

A Home Is Made Of Hopes And Dreams

A home is made of hopes and dreams,
Not doors, walls nor lights,
And life measured by moments lived,
Not passing days and nights.

Only then do we truly live,
Each moment that comes our way,
That's what I think dear reader,
Tell me what you have to say.

Hopes and dreams are the substance,
Of that which keeps us going,
East, West, North and South,
As we keep toing and froing,

Hope springs eternal
In the human breast,
Despair puts man
Through a severe test.

One thing more that's always true,
Everything in life is not about me and you.

21.

Restore Sanity To Man, O Lord

Restore sanity to man, O Lord,
Let him primitive be again,
For even with his axe and tool,
He never caused his neighbour pain.

A jungle now of a different kind
Is the world of today,
The battle now between man and man,
For he has lost his way.

The carnivores of old no more,
What roams the streets now,
Is a power-hungry voracious being,
That maims and loots, and how!

Such is the maze of materialism
Where dust masquerades as gold,
Values that man once held so dear
Now on permanent hold.

Skies will be dark and sometimes blue,
So it is with dreams,
With rills and with little streams,
They meld and vanish with the sea,
For that is but their destiny,
The end of all journeys is nothing
But Eternity.

22.

What Is Grief And What Loss?

What is grief and what loss
When nothing is truly ever ours?
For all we have is the life we're blessed with,
No mansions, no palaces, no bowers.

When the stay itself is transient
What possessions can we lay claim to?
And, since the purpose of life is happiness,
Let's live it without much ado.

And to be and stay just happy
Is itself an art we must learn,
Think of the times you felt despair
And how things then began to turn.

Nothing must ever be taken for granted,
For nothing was meant to last,
Just look at the things we thought once ours,
That now belong to the past.

No one but you can take away
That lovely smile you possess,
Nor ever the glow of God's light within,
So why hanker for more or settle for less?

23.

Relentlessly The Sun At Dawn Rose

Relentlessly the sun at dawn rose,
The wide-eyed star understands and knows,
Ere into oblivion it reluctantly goes,
Nothing lasts or forever grows.

And night too slain by day,
Put to rest by the sun's first ray,
What is there to feel or say,
When the mood is sombre, dark and grey.?

But the star and night they both know,
They have no other place to go,
The journey fast or ever so slow,
Their destiny is the to and fro.

For fate does put all to test,
And does so with zeal and zest,
And like the wave at its crest,
It does but all lay to rest.

So worry not, O anxious man,
Live happily so long as you can,
You too will breast the tape one day,
However fast or slow you ran.

24.
How Fake The World Today

Fake is bonhomie, fake the smiles,
Snooping, cheating the real things,
Blackened hearts and icy stares,
This is what progress seemingly brings.

Honest feelings and honest words,
Left behind and lost somewhere,
Bank Street where heaven is,
But fake notes won't get you there!!

Fake is the new mantra now,
All because the gods have changed,
Mammon truly rules the roost,
And Man truly now deranged.

Clouds now in man's grasp,
Computing as he does his life,
Whoever does with Nature spend
Moments without some kind of strife?

Fake it all while you can,
For Death is real, O pitiable man.

25.

Heavenly Moments

Each one's heaven is one's own,
So go and find your own too,
It may be something very simple,
A drop of water might just do,
If thirst is what is killing you.

Imagine a tiger facing you,
You'll be in rigor, that is true,
A shaft of lightning from the sky,
Strikes the tiger and you don't die.
Who sent that flash down for you,
Out of nowhere, out of the blue,
And why?
Just a heavenly hand on the sly.

A sip of tea in a sylvan setting,
A tête-à-tête with a fireside ember,
Moments that you oft remember,
Were they not enthralling times,
Those childhood days, those sing-song rhymes?

Heavenly times is what heaven is,
Looking skywards is futile biz,
A happy mind and disposition
And heaven always in your grasp,
A thorn in the side, a bit like hell,
But remember,
Heaven's in your hand, when a rose you clasp.

26.
Human Nature

Tell me someone tell me true,
Is human nature so very base,
That envy is the primal force,
That drives us all in life's zigzag race?

And strangers better than the known here,
Cos love and care don't mean much,
Covetous hearts are shallow indeed,
And lose the beauty of another's touch.

Can we not in another's joy,
Partake without the jealous dart?
What kind of man does that need?
What kind of mind, what kind of heart?

Is it naive to believe,
That goodness always will prevail?
And every story always end,
As does every little fairy tale?

We may be brighter, bigger and richer too,
Than whose who went before us,
But are we better human beings,
For me it's a minus, not a plus.

27.
O, How Awful Is Routine

O, how we all hate routine
And love variety,
To spice up life and then
Seek constant ecstasy.

Repetition is, O, so boring,
And 'newness' so divine,
Why should I then be slave to
Thing or thought when each breath is mine?

And did you never realize
How routine it is to breathe,
And if heartbeat isn't regular,
In rigor you would writhe?

So don't decry monotony,
Routine is most of life,
Eat, drink and merry be,
And surely you'll beat strife.

28.
The Pursuit of Happiness

If happiness you find in unhappiness
Would you then yourself unhappy make,
Beat and bruise the soul and mind
And to debilitating masochism take?

What pleasure can this anyone give?
Redemption, maybe, to closeted guilt?
But lasting joy and happiness true
Is never on slippery sands built.

Even if destiny is not your creed
And that pillar of hope you pillory,
Remember, each one lives a life their own,
And is then consigned to memory.

Don't shelter take in pleasure false,
Ephemeral is never the happy state,
Happiness is a just state of mind,
And nothing to do with fame, love or hate.

29.
When Twilight Does Its Shadows Cast

When twilight does its shadows cast,
I know that nothing does for ever last,
Each day gives way to a blissful night,
As darkness does to dawn and light.

Each beat of the heart is a heartbeat less
Than the number with which He did me bless,
Life knows in whose arms it will end,
Cos to the will of the lord, life must bend.

No worry, no care does childhood carry,
Nor queries does it ever parry,
Answers to all questions, folks
Are all left to dear old Uncle Harry.

The pursuit of happiness must the goal be,
All else is mirage, unfortunately,
And for that which lies only within you,
Where else will you look, isn't that true,
But within you?

30.
Bygones

When I see these shoots of green,
I am in the midst of that sylvan scene,
When all around me were forests deep,
And by the river I fell asleep.

As it quietly flowed on its way,
So as not to wake me as I lay,
The whispers from those little waves,
Were moments that memory saves.

For days and times such as these
Where are those woods and where that breeze?
Now with the aid of resting dreams,
Tucked away somewhere in little streams.

In the labyrinths of the mind,
Oft have I softly tread,
To look for things, to somehow find,
That which I have left behind,
That which has but passed me by.

Are these those stars in the sky,
The ones with whom I spent my nights?
Is this the sky that in the day,
Gave me space to fly my kites?

Or have they too like me of old
By Time, been down the river sold?

For Time the healer,
The wheeler-dealer,
Kind and savage all in one,
Who has ever Time out-run?

Bow we must to Time and age,
So said the fool and the sage,
However full my book of life,
Over time it is but an empty page.

31.
Beauty Does Envy Invite

Beauty does envy invite,
And brains both wrath and scorn,
Lucky then the plain fool,
Who with neither is luckily born!

Luck favours the plain then
So what use those handsome looks?
And when happy is the simpleton
What use those mighty books?

Careful sifting of all facts,
Is what the wise do,
Rationalize then re-rationalize,
Isn't that true for you?

I'd rather lucky and happy be,
To hoots with Relativity,
So handsome was Narcissus,
A watery grave was his destiny.

But looks or no looks I'll happy be,
For that is life for me, you see.

32.
Flight of Mind

When my mind does to the heavens soar,
Boundless are both Time and Space,
No wings do I but ever need,
And greased lightning is my pace.

By my side is the star I choose,
The moon not far away,
The Earth I see just a tiny dot,
No sea, no shore, no bay.

In the vastness of that emptiness
All else is small like me,
Cos nothing is greater than a 'nothingness',
That embraces all it can see.

And then my mind free like a bird
Swishes, swoops and sways,
Conjuring up images of heaven and more,
In a million, myriad, ways.

The hell on earth I then lay to rest
On the bed of cloud near my feet,
And wallow I do in ecstasy
And marvel at my feat.

O flight of mind I salute thee,
For you set me free, eternally.

33.
Never Say Die

Watch the battered little stooping flower
The fury of the skies face,
For that must the motto be
Of those who run in life's race.

Hurdles will astrewn lie,
Willy-nilly on your way,
And like the flower you must too
Rise, the very next day.

Cos that is what the night is for,
Your weariness to remove,
To get you ready for the battle ahead,
To get you in the groove.

Never-say-die as long as you live,
Why give it more than its due?
O Death, you are no more than the end of life,
Isn't that quite simply true?

The spirit of Man must never flag,
Drooping flowers will never do,
However little the flower I saw,
In my esteem it vastly grew.
And taught me the lesson I shall never rue.
Never Say Die.

34.
The Arrogant Scavenger

I want to live and you can't take me away,
Not until I give you the say,
Not until I tire of life
Will I let you in to have your way.

God and I have a strange pact
Go ask Him if that's not a fact,
He is my Master and yours too,
Without His consent even you can't act.

My pact with Him is simply this,
Whenever you ask He'll give you the miss,
O Death, you will not understand,
My deal with Him ensures me bliss.

When He and I the day decide,
I'll let you in for the final ride,
For you to transport me then,
And take me to with Him reside.

I pity the arrogance that you display
The rites, the wreaths, memorials too,
And having done with one,
You'll go looking for others,
Won't you?

Remember,
Those that do things remove,
Are called scavengers,
On the move.

35.
Blessings

May your skies be clear and blue,
Your nights and days forever true,
Your words and deeds always such,
That you never have to anything rue.

May you never have to stoop or bend,
Or 'sorrys' to anyone ever send,
But should you need to then you must,
To a winner be, at the end.

May you never have to pain endure,
May the steps you take be firm and sure,
May your train of thought that never ends,
Pass through a filter, emerge pure.

May joy always pave the way,
May you be blessed at work and play,
May roses in your garden grow, and,
These blessings keep all thorns away.

When uneven is the path you tread,
Keep your cool, keep your head,
No panic do you ever need,
Keep hope and faith alive instead.

Find your ways to peace of mind,
Else you will be to yourself unkind,
You are important to yourself, but,
To the needs of others, never be blind.

36.

Thank God for Mercies All

Mercies all big and small
Lessen the impact of every fall,
For were it not for His benediction,
Unbearable would be the human affliction.

Benign is all He ever does,
His wrath too has a melodic buzz,
For when it all comes crashing down.
He still won't let you helplessly drown.

Light He will the paths for you,
And darkness lift, this is true,
However dim the glimmer of hope,
He'll give you the will to heal and cope.

Could have been worse is always possible,
Would have been worse, the better thought,
To keep you from depression away,
To let you not in misery wallow,
To help you bear and peaceful stay.

37.
Beyond All Barriers

What hurdles can we ever place
In the paths of a soaring bird?
Indomitable is the human spirit,
And that is the describing word.

Beyond all barriers of Time and Space
Does the spirit and mind of Man,
Explore all lands, the skies and more,
For nothing will stop it nor can.

Like the Phoenix that does from the ashes rise,
To glory seek relentlessly,
Never say die the immortal motto,
That Man carries eternally.

No barriers then can ever hold back,
The soaring human spirit,
For beyond all barriers does it lie,
And freedom we must give it.

38.

Is There An Art To Fading Away?

There must be an art to fading away,
For who can for ever in the limelight stay,
When thorns begin to their presence flaunt,
On paths that roses once lined the way?

Arc lights are nice but dazzling too,
And fame holds the lamp, that's also true,
But remember the time will also come,
When the very same lights will dazzle, but only you.

And like the rose that has had its day
As king of the show both bright and gay,
Must we all learn to deftly drop
The colourful petals, and let Time have its say.

Reconciliation then the only way
For peace of mind, at both work and play,
But, O, how difficult it is to treat
Each dawn as another restful, relaxing Sunday.

39.

Contentment

Drifting sands and foreign lands,
Are appealing to the heart,
But the stable shore and the homely mart,
Bring warmth and cheer to the heart.

Dazzling lights and spires tall,
Are yours to only see,
Like shadows that we in futility chase,
Like mirages in the mind, some place.

Contentment lies in the inner self,
In the worn-out chair and shoe,
And not for long does the lustre last
Of that which is brand new.

That which we can call our own
Is music to the ears,
Like laughter shared and tears spent,
Like happy hearts and honest intent.

40.
The Mind

Enslave me, put me through the grind,
But subjugate me you can never,
For free I am like the bird on high,
In the expanse of a boundless sky.

Depths I plumb and zenith attain,
To the stars and back in a twinkle,
Time and space at my beck and call,
No fear, no cares at all.

I bear my crosses with fortitude,
And that is true no doubt,
But repair I can and quickly too
Myself, and that is also true.

Faster than anything known for speed,
I travel far and wide,
And when you think the master you are,
I can take you for a ride.

Rational and irrational both,
Believer and agnostic too,
Strange mix of contradiction,
Dark and grey and blue.

And that, dear reader, is the Mind,
Dissected for you.

41.

Love God Don't Fear Him

You can bow your head in faith or fear,
The choice entirely yours,
Fear God or love Him, as you please,
Without dogmas, without mores.

Fear will keep you fearful
Of retribution for things done wrong,
But love will in your heart
Sing His praise, sans song.

Those that you truly care for,
Their faults you recognize,
Cos weakness is a human trait,
You have them too, so be wise.

And if God you love and not fear,
You know it from the start,
Mercy you will surely receive,
Cos He is benevolent at heart.

42.

The Salt Of The Earth

Salt, O Gibran, is not in our tears,
Nor is it in the vast and open seas,
The sweat of the brow is the salt of the earth,
And from it, its salt, it receives.

The true worth of salt always is,
The lives we try and emulate,
Those qualities that we hold precious
Are what make it sacred and great.

Sincerity, Amity, Love and Toil,
The first letters do the word salt read,
And these are what makes salt dear to us,
And these are all we need

To live a life of fulfilment.
Why waste salt on tears?
An honest day's work is all we need,
To banish from the mind, our fears.

43.
The Mirage Called Peace

Will we ever true peace achieve
With different faiths across the world?
How will 'Good' the 'Evil' banish,
When acrimony is freely hurled?

When God is one for one and all
Why do we not, just Him adore?
And on the pillars of man-made faiths,
Stop looking for points to score.

No peace till all these faiths last
Someone said some time ago,
Is this true I often wonder,
Do faiths help us live, before we go?

'Tis for each one to think and ponder,
Who or what is greater, God or religion?
Else peace will lie beyond the wild blue yonder
Shimmering waves, the desire for unison.

O what a hypocritical world we live in, Ashok,
Where arms you need to maintain peace,
The irony of it is laughable indeed,
When everyone is out to the other fleece.

44.
To The Women Of The World

Think fulfilment not empowerment
And you'll better then succeed,
To attain what you wish to
And fulfil your every need.

The word empowerment is so macho
So alien to the beautiful you,
Why must you then this garb wear,
And to yourself, dear lady, be untrue?

No hackles would you raise,
Nor undue obstacles face,
If fulfilment is you motto
Man would help you win the race.

No one leaves a battle unscarred,
Bodies maimed and egos bruised,
The clarion call for empowerment has,
Left a 'weak' man confused.

By a simple substitution
If your goal you achieve,
Why wouldn't you simply do that,
And accolades receive?

45.

Are Faiths Stable?

If stable is the belief in faiths,
Why do we proselytize?
If God is one and universal,
Why different to different eyes?

Do faiths offer unique potions
What else could be the charm?
For believers to ride different horses,
To save themselves from wrath and harm.

Surely He designed it better,
Surely He's not a mix
Of all the faiths that thrive on earth,
Surely that's not His fix.

Then how does one faith proclaim
Its infallibility,
Promises make to its adherents all,
To help them find eternity?

The hand of Man is more apparent
Than, perhaps, it outwardly seems,
For carpet-baggers do charmingly sell
Mirages and empty dreams.

No different road to heaven
Does any faith prescribe,
Cos God is one for all and sundry,
And that's the lesson to imbibe.

46.

Just Ruminating

In the illusory world of pomp and glory,
Have I friendships sometimes lost,
Do I even know for sure,
If that is true and at what cost?

Will my friendship with myself
In my favour tilt the scales,
Is the ship that's safely anchored
Safer than the one that sails?

Are all battles singly fought
And armies all the strength of one?
The General and the soldier too,
All within when it's finished and done.

Must all questions have an answer?
Why must I all-knowing be?
Why can't I simply rise and set
As does the sun and smilingly?

47.
Dreams

Are dreams no more than smouldering fire,
The flames of hope but dying ember,
Like the colours that line autumnal paths,
That soon give way to the blizzards of December?

Or is night the true reality
And the phantom of dawn, the illusive day,
Does the garb of darkness light reveal,
And daylight act the interim play?

Is sleep then the natural state
And wakefulness an aberration?
Nocturnal times the eternal balm
All else no more than just sensation?

Is Subconscious then the real thing,
And Consciousness just plain bling?

48.
The Beauty Of The Unknown

Ripples in the pond and waves in the sea,
Little steps, giant strides of an unknown destiny,
But that is the beauty of life, after all,
For what would be the point, if mirrored on the wall?

The unknown it is that gives rise to dreams,
To reach the stars and test extremes,
To challenge yourself on paths anew,
And give you the courage to try and do.

To believe in the self and the spirit of Man,
Aided by destiny to do what he can,
For strive we must then hope for the best,
And remember that each one goes through the test.

Thank God we don't know what lies ahead,
Or else life would be as good as dead.

49.
A Clean Mind

We must from our minds the cobwebs remove,
That have made a home there,
The fertile mind ploughed and ravaged by Time,
When the seeds of Prejudice,
Arrogance, Discrimination , Anger and Greed,
Find no quarter,
Thrive Not.
Where noble, gentle, strains of thought shall for ever reign,
And,
The colour green our colour be.

No,
Not the green of Envy,
But the green that Nature bestows on Man,
The green of the trees,
The green of the leaves,
The green that is the shoot of Life,
Plantings that the sun adores,
A wholesome set of values and mores,
How green then would our valleys be,
And rivers flow to the eternal sea.

A clean mind is a cleansed soul,
No parts, just whole.

The rusted carapace peeled off,
The falsity of Time exposed,
Contretemps,
A foreign word,

That never again will its ugly head raise,
Lowered for ever
To meld with dust.

That field of thought we must plant,
We must,
For only then will we be free,
From want, from misery.

50.

Sorry

Sorry only when it's from the heart,
Too glib for me is just the tongue,
What grief is ever truly expressed,
When the eyes are tearless as a dirge is sung?

Try cover the truth all you like,
The eyelids will never the truth hide,
No veil can keep shame hidden for long,
The eyes will reveal the words that lied.

The heart has its reasons we all know that,
Some we do and some don't understand,
Great is the belief in humility,
For you see then the Unseen 'omni' hand.

Forgive and forgiveness seek
And a calm contented soul you'll be,
Seek and you shall always receive,
Blessings and His unfailing mercy.

51.

Hear The Whispers Of The Rill

Hear the whispers of the rill
Until,
Of that little stream
That little dream,
You've had your fill,
And,

Swayed by the breeze
In step with the leaves,
You fly to the clouds,
And at the stars gaze,

Through mist and haze,
Then see the Earth from afar
See how small you really are,
When face you do a heavenly star,
And then,

Your place is what you get to know,
Your place in the sun is but a dot,
The world you see is all a show
No big, no small,
One size fits all,
When you look within
Afar from din,
You get to see the real you.

How warped is the human mind today,
Contentment being a foreign word,
Peace within and without
A vagrant mythical restive bird.

Guns and bombs are the keepers of peace,
Irony at its eloquent best,
Man's very survival, O Lord, at stake,
And put to the severest test.

52.
Melancholia

Melancholia in the psyche,
Masochistic in parts,
Are we designed to hurt ourselves?
Shed pity in fits and starts?

'Poor little me's' a forsaken self,
Even God's left me out,
Doesn't look my way, heed my call,
I'm bereft of divine clout.

To whom do I turn in distress,
For no one listens to me?
Let me beat myself a little,
Bleed a little and see.

I might gain sympathy
A shoulder find to cry on,
Pour my heart out, exaggerate,
Then find the shoulder's gone,
To leave me where I wish to be,
Wallowing in my misery.

But, O Wallower, there's another way,
And a better one for sure,
Go look yourself in the eye,
Feel sorry for self no more.

Cos no one's better than another,
For equal are we made,
The mightiest too do sometimes feel,
They too have been had and laid.

So you 'poor little me', you rotten sod,
Get up and show the world,
No more is it than a lump of earth,
With fanfare unfurled.

Take your mind off your wretched self
Go take a giant stride,
Pat yourself on your broad back,
And never yourself deride.

Melancholy can be a lovely tune,
But only in doses small,
Lost loves and times bring some smiles back,
But never grovel, always stand tall.

53.
Life Is Futile Without Hope

Life is futile without hope,
Dull and dreary without dreams,
If the thought of tomorrow's dawn
Does nothing more than make you yawn.

It's a sad day my friend,
If all you're doing
Is simply waiting for the inevitable end.

When the morning glow of the rising sun
That shimmers across the ocean blue,
Does nothing to lift the spirits up,
Of a rested but hope-less you,

When zephyr
Does its easterly blow,
And you have but no place to go,
No need, no want, no desire at all,
Then you are ready to stumble,
To fall.

The spark within must always burn,
Brightly too, before the urn,
Or else,
Dust will meet dust for sure,
That is true for evermore.

But while you live
To yourself you must give
The will, the reason, to carry on,

To climb the mountain and sail the seas,
To let the mind go with the breeze
And you can do this with ease,

If the lamp of Hope you extinguish not,
Don't run from the sun when it's truly hot,
Face the heat and beat it too,
And to yourself be always true.

For you can fool the world for a while,
With what you think is clever guile,
But, on reflection, you will see,
The only one fooled is the one called 'me'.

The 'me' you see in a looking-glass,
Is brutally frank and revealing,
For nothing's hidden from the one you know best,
You,
Try it out, it's a simple test.

But whatever you do, look ahead,
For the past is long gone, dead,
And that is where the hope of morrow's light,
Helps you pass a weary night,

And it's that candle of hope that flickers on,
That you must carry in your heart,
From beginning to the end,
As on Life's stage
You play your part,
Till the curtain falls and you,
Like the rest,
Depart.

54.
Why Do We Tremble At The Thought Of Our Demise

Why do we tremble at the thought of our demise
And yet are labelled bright and worldly-wise?
And then a day well spent ends,
With regret, remorse and sadly, sighs,

Proud, haughty and all-knowing,
Beseeching mercy from the skies,
Why do tears bring relief
To seemingly happy dancing eyes?
And why is simple, honest, unyielding truth,
Enwrapped in convoluted, twisted lies?

We focus on vain results
Whatever happened to efforts and tries?
Are gods just spectators now
Prayers mere distraught cries?

Cos man's lost his way, alas!
Midst fast food and crunchy fries,
And powered by arrogance
Even His existence denies,
He dreams of immortality
And never ending mortal ties,

No warmth, no feeling
In today's nonchalant 'Hi's',
And the less said the better of hurriedly said goodbyes,
Where all that matters is to smother
The 'Noes' and gobble up the 'Ayes'.

How strange the world today,
Where all we do is chastise,
Curse our fate and then,
Throughout life, grumble and agonize.

55.
The Drifting Clouds, The Sailing Birds

The drifting clouds, the sailing birds,
And I run out of simple words,
To paint the picture of an ethereal morn,
The orange glow, the break of dawn.

As the night, that ally of dreams and sleep,
Has promises to others to also keep,
For them too to weariness shed,
And, like me, awaken from the land of the dead.

For night and sleep are both friends and foes,
And who but Morpheus better knows,
The land of quiet and the land of dreams,
Where the ships are yours, as are the streams,

To sail up or down the silent rill,
Or the beauty watch as you lie still,
And in the quiet that is the night,
Demons see or angels sight.

For the mind's eye needs no light,
Other than what we call insight,
From consciousness we are then freed,
Both in word and in deed.

To do with the mind as we please,
To let it rest or climb the trees,
And perched thus up on high,
Shake the hand of the sky.

Then say goodnight or goodbye,
For ramble you can but only thus far,
For rambling beyond this, Ashok,
Will only begin to slowly jar.

56.

If It Was Not For Peers

If it was not for peers
And not for seers
Would life then more pleasurable be?
Insanity then would rule the day,
Man free to have his every say
In the throes of unchained ecstasy.

Insane we are in equal measure
For sanity is but half the treasure,
The 'madness' of dervishes we all see,
And the sins we commit.
When inflamed and 'lit'.
Are the stuff of infamy and history.

For good reason then are we bound
For we know the jungle is a place unsound
For never should we trust the untrustworthy,
Cos we all know what animals are,
And man from them is not very far.

Bereft of the chains of morality,
Outdated is the currency of modesty,
Overpowered as we are by raw passion
More so today cos that is the fashion.
Whatever happened to values old
When dust was never sold as gold,
No sleight of hand, no alchemy.

Life is and can devastating be
And this is not said jokingly,

For we all know what it is, don't we?
How naive we are, O gentle folks,
To believe life's troubles are no more than hoax.
And this, Ashok, is no homily.

57.
The Crimson Hibiscus

How does crimson turn to ruddy black,
With the afternoon sun on its back,
Ask my red hibiscus, will you?
And every word you'll find is true.

Cos with every dawn and its dew,
The only colours are red, green and blue,
For the flower, the grass and the mighty sky,
Are the only things that meet my eye,
Until to the Orb and its majesty,
All manner of life submits, humbly,
And my hibiscus too, just like me,
Succumbs,
And what's left of crimson is what I see.

Then meld it does with the night,
As I bid it adieu in fading light,
For never again shall I see it,
As each leaf of the flower falls, bit by bit.

And that's the story of my lovely flower,
That lives its life by the hour,
And in its wake for me a lesson leaves.

Rejoice in my being,
Cos only the fool grieves.

58.

The River And I

Live and die by the river,
Midst the sounds of the birds,
Where silence is pure beatitude,
Why pollute it with empty words.

The sounds I hear are heavenly,
The mind at ease and calm,
For the anguished, tortured, restless soul,
The river is the elusive balm.

Flow it does but, gently,
Still, as is the beating heart,
Coursing through both valley and hill,
Every dawn a vibrant start.

O, River, you do but symbolize,
The way we should all live our lives,
Ripples, waves and the storms you face,
The destiny too of the human race.

But seldom do we realize,
The shadows that walk by our side,
Bright and dark and uneven paths,
Are there for all in life's ride.

So envy not another soul,
Cos every being is less than whole,
Hope your mirror tells you, brother,
You're no better than any other.

59.
Dahlias, Hibiscus, Cinerarias

Dahlias, hibiscus, cinerarias,
Petunias, pansies, nasturtium and lilies too,
Midst this riot of colour, radiance and beauty
I sometimes see
A pensive, morose me,
But only sometimes,
For I am mostly like
What I choose to see, and be.

Cos the power of distinction does lie within,
Light from dark
And,
Cloud from rainbow,
Night from Day,
And rye from hay,
Truth from a lie
And the pie in the sky,
These are things that make me glad,
These are things that make me sad,
And between the two
Are tears of joy,
The morning mist and drops of dew.

Why does a word have meanings two?
Why is blue not always blue?

60.

Ignorance Is Bliss

If ignorance is bliss
Then it's folly to be wise,
So let's learn to live happily
With our ignorant 'highs'.

With tongues so glib
What doesn't meet the eyes,
More often than not
May be a pack of lies.

Competition is fierce
And the world a 'high-rise',
Look at man reaching out
To outdo the skies,

Forgotten the beauty of that which is low,
Like snow on the ground and glowing sunrise,
O what a pitiable, delusional world,
And yet we lay claim to be worldly-wise.

61.
Try Selling A 'Good' Newspaper

Try selling a 'good' newspaper
And you will surely come a cropper.
Are we then designed as humans,
To savour the thrill of the improper?

Exhorted by the Commandments,
To refrain and walk the narrow,
To abstain from all that's illicit,
And not pick and flit like the sparrow.

Bound by chains of morality,
And the script of right and wrong,
To break free is the desire,
And for that does man long?

The devil too once an angel,
Whose fall from heaven is well known,
Are the seeds for evil in man
From birth, willy-nilly, sown?

Questions eternal, eternally there,
The answers not easy to find,
Theories aplenty and seers afloat,
But the truth in each one's mind.

Sort out for yourself the muddle,
And a muddle it is, my friends,
A maze is a conundrum remember,
A beginning with no ends.

62.

The River And The Sea

Who is the more eager of the two
The river or the sea,
The one to a destination reach,
The other to add to eternity?

The conundrum's there for you to see,
Life like a train at breakneck speed
Hurtling towards its destiny,
Without caution, without heed.

And the 'end' there in waiting mode,
Knowing that which only it knows,
All that comes by its nature own,
By that nature, in time, goes.

Like the sea and the river,
It's all in the hands of the Eternal Giver.

63.

Sycophants

Are we all not sycophants?
Choosing 'tween God and man,
Whom to please when and why,
The one on the ground or the one in the sky,

Appease we do and please too.
In a myriad forms and ways,
Both the Lord and mortal man,
Prostrating, the common craze.

To power does man always bend,
Supreme or temporal no matter, friend,
For weak in spirit and flesh is he,
Cos that for mortals is destiny.

Man prays to God for forgiveness and mercy,
And seeks it from his own too,
Currying favour with both equally,
Hedging bets he's known to do.

Inscrutable the ways of the Almighty,
And strange those of Man.

64.
Is Destiny Mirage?

Is destiny real or hallucination?
Ridden with controversy and fascination
Does fate lie with the stars above,
Where is He, the God I love?

Must truth strike me between the eyes,
For me to lift the lid off lies?
Must trees when bare the chance seize
To tell the world they have leaves?

Must faith and belief move beyond song?
What is not right, must it be wrong?
Must queries and doubts torment the mind,
And we spend lives to answers find?

Can't we just live and die,
And do so with no more than a sigh?
Leave the suffering of remorse, regret and the past,
At the bottom of the to-do list, last.

Cos nothings worse than to chastise the self,
Not even the taint of sullied pelf,
For Time treats all in equal measure,
And every moment is life's only treasure.

For once at least, O Lord, appear
To mortal eyes then disappear,
For it's only me that needs to see,
For the rest it is their destiny.

But digressed I have from the subject at hand,
For uneven it is the lie of that land,
Ten times a day do I believe
And five, O Lord, wish to perceive,
You.

Cos that is how you have made me,
To put it straight and simply.

65.

The Ocean of Bewilderment

Oft have I bewildered stood,
Alone on a desolate shore,
No boat in sight nor traveller,
Unaware of what's in store.

The vastness of the ocean blue,
And I the grain of sand,
So dark the contrast 'tween ocean and me,
How little I know and less understand.

Like an orphaned drop of the wave,
Torn from its roots for ever,
Lost in the sands of Time,
To return to the seas but never.

Then from that shore have I walked away,
With emptiness in tow,
That which I felt in the ocean's sway,
Its ebb and tide and flow.

The reality of life dawns on us,
When time we give to it,
Shallow and deep are ends both,
That cross we must, dark or lit.

66.

O Beautiful Sleep

Do monsters of the deep conspire
To keep me from my sleep?
There is no smoke, no smouldering fire,
Why then do I lie awake and weep?

How long can I the stars count
For soon it will be morn,
The rays of light, the sun's fount,
And I'm lost and forlorn.

Will another night my ally be
Will Morpheus come to my aid?
For I'd like to close my eyes, not see,
Another night un-made.

Sleep, not dreams, am I looking for,
Not greedily ambitious am I,
Simple to the very core,
Not reaching for the sky.

Why then am I deprived of sleep
When I ask for nothing more,
Tell me Life, cos from you I'm derived,
Will I tonight be with the one I adore?
My sleep.

67.

Delicate Is The Gentle String

Delicate is the gentle string,
That keeps us bound together,
More so in the world of today,
Where friends are like fair weather.

Bonding is a 'virtual' word
But it takes more than empty space,
To fill the gaps and keep the whole,
In the lifelong 'bonding' race.

For very little does it take,
To tear the fabric apart,
An unkind look or a word that's harsh,
Can rip the kindest heart.

Be wary then of what you say or do
Cos understanding is all,
For little does it take to jeopardize
A kind notion, for you to stumble and fall.

The heart has strings we all know that,
So be careful with the one you pull,
Remember the glass that to you is empty,
May well be more than half full.

68.
Even Angels Are Known To Cry

O, the pitter-patter of raindrops,
From mournful teary skies,
Who said the heavens never wept,
Don't angels too have eyes?

Why label crying as such a shame
When tears help cleanse the soul?
Of remorse and regret and searing grief,
For who is ever whole?

When a dam is close to bursting
It's wise to open the gates,
To relieve the built-up pressure,
Before it escalates,

A good laugh and a good cry then
Are cathartic and should assist,
To balance the scales of emotion,
So why would you then, either resist?

69.

Fly Against The Flock

Fly Against the flock
Or run with the herd,
Success follows failure,
Perseverance is the word,

A drop's no more than a drop,
For alone an ocean it can't make,
But it's there and always ready,
To join others, for the ocean's sake,

Strike out on your own if you will,
But a one-man army's no match,
For the cohesion that teamwork builds,
Encouraged, you won't floor the catch.

Togetherness is the watchword,
The mantra that bails us out,
The principles of harmony,
You should never, but never, flout.

Birds of a feather flock together
And do so for good reason,
Spring today and autumn tomorrow,
But never forget the winter season.

70.
Distraught Mind

A distraught mind is best suited for peace,
Cos it needs that most,
Like a ship in turmoil searching for,
The anchor of the coast.

Like a barren tree in winter's grip
Shorn of leaves that warmth provide,
A grieving mind does body and soul,
Relentlessly divide.

Like windswept lands and desert too,
Convulsed is the mind by storms its own,
A rocking boat in great distress,
A field where nothing but weed is sown.

Deep within its recesses,
Like furrowed lands there lie,
Grooves, wrinkles and the like,
Invisible to the human eye.

The healing touch and balm then
Is just plain empathy?
A kind word, a helping hand,
Understanding and sympathy.

No sermons needed, no censure too,
For the mind that's adrift and this is true.

71.

The Other Side of Dark Is Light

The other side of dark is light
Would there a day be if there was no night?
Look at love then at hate,
They are prone to willy-nilly, mate!

Look at winter, chill and all,
Compensated by a nippy fall,
The devil I may be, and you?
Remember Satan was an angel too.

And ships that sail the stormy seas,
In balmier times do as they please.
To what would you aspire if there was no hell?
And what would be life without the tolling bell?

Truth is meaningless without the lie,
Vision is but the mind's eye,
The heart will beat, until,
Life hums and,
Then goes still.

72.

Life Is A Winding Road

Dawn to dusk is a winding road,
That we with uncertainty tread,
Each step do we with trepidation take,
And then the night we dread.

Afraid of light and scared of dark,
The mind in great turmoil,
Our storms do we ourselves create,
With what we believe is guile.

The mind does but games play,
With each of us in the field,
Mostly netting an own goal,
With a mind that should be a shield.

The worst that can happen to us,
Is the end called demise,
But why do we invite daily,
Annihilation with open eyes?

I remind myself of the lines above,
As often as I possibly can,
I know I too will breast the tape,
However my race I ran.

There is no such thing as a life eternal,
And eternity you will reach,
But only after you're done with life,
Is the lesson that life does teach.

73.
My Name Is Pretty Winter

Why do you look at me disconsolately,
When warmth is all I provide?
You wouldn't be there but for me,
You wouldn't be by the fireside.

My name is Pretty Winter,
I am clad in snow that's white,
Pure and chaste, untouched,
By the harshness of summer's might.

The mountains love me much,
And you ski down the slopes, don't you?
'Tis for Nature and Man that I'm around,
But the brunt of my temper you bear, that's true.

But there is a softer side to me,
My heart too does melt,
I've seen my trees bereft of leaves,
Their penury I have felt.

I can be mild and gentle,
When I see you withered and worn,
And summon then what follows
The Spring, yet to see the break of dawn.

If it wasn't for my chill, my friend,
You'd never know what 'woollies' are,
And it's only when you're summer-struck,
Am I, for the course, then par.

I suffer the cold too, you know,
In silence and in wait,
So please don't be harsh and dismissive,
Cos I deserve a better fate.

I shan't be severe I promise,
If you promise to not give me a miss,
I'll be back from my sabbatical,
To give you, as does a cold mistress,
A blistering warm kiss!!

74.
Half Moon

O half moon, so neatly halved,
Never have I seen you thus in the sky,
Are you the one playing games with me,
Or, is it my deceiving eye?

Perhaps I will the stars ask
If they see you differently,
Do they see the better half,
Are you clad with modesty?

Your glowing face all aglow,
But what's the other side,
For it's dark and I can't really see,
And to your beauty am I tied.

But get back to being whole please,
For halves leave much to be desired.

75.

Tears Are No Balm For The Parched Soul

Tears are no balm for the parched soul,
Remorse helps but does not make it whole,
For guilt in the heart will not wash away,
Moral transgression leads to decay,

For the spirit once tarred is for ever stained,
And fragile like glass we know,
Cracks in the mirror for ever there,
Repaired well, but still won't go.

Few did ever from example learn,
And sermons are but futile,
Universal is the learning curve,
And it takes each one a while.

If weeds you grow in your garden
Weeds you will admire,
But to have a bed of roses,
To a garden you must aspire.

76.

Misfortune Does A Lesson Hide

From misfortune must I always learn,
To never let that journey fruitless be,
For the darkest night however long,
Will, in time, the sunrise see.

Flowers that blossom in my garden,
Will to Nature succumb too,
Plants will droop and fade away,
As I too will numb and so will you.

But from the days of sweat and toil,
And a frowning destiny,
Must I like the Phoenix rise,
From the ashes, mysteriously.

Like the river that runs a destined course,
O'er rock and crag and smooth alike,
To meet the sea and eternity,
I too, must on my own strike.

Each fall is followed by a rise,
And Spring does the Winter bury,
I too will carry a cheerful heart,
A cheerful smile and be merry.

77.
The Bolt From The Blue

The flicker of lightning that I see,
And the smell of rain in the air,
Leave the soul but vulnerable,
All emotions laid bare.

As if the falling tears from above,
Mirror the image of my heart,
For what I feel and also see,
Is both pleasure and pain, in part.

The bolt from the blue is awesome indeed,
No more than just a flash,
Hand in hand with raging thunder,
It does fatally strike and crash.

The fear in its wake is palpable,
To its majesty do I then bow,
For to Nature did the Almighty,
Enormous power endow.

78.
Desire

O how immortal is the soul,
And how fatal is desire,
Are we designed to fall prey
And be consumed by fire?

Is the spirit truly divine,
And the flesh mortally weak?
Does the devil reside within us,
Is man's future ominously bleak?

Or is desire the needed engine,
That locomotion provides,
To the spirit that resides within us,
And not that which us divides?

Is desire just temptation?
Or, does there lie within it,
Man's salvation, Ashok,
And tell me, if desire is divine writ?

Is it dark and dangerous,
Or, does it the spirit lift?
Is it the abode of Satan,
Or, is it God's gift?

79.

What Transformation Has Taken Place?

What transformation has taken place?
Soundlessly, silently, someone tell me,
Why do I not feel the same now,
What is this strange mystery?

Can't be the clouds I flew over,
Nor the stars that lit up the sky,
If you're happy with the change,
Dear fellow,
Why look for the reasons, why?

There is much beyond comprehension,
The human mind no match for Nature,
Pygmy is Man in comparison,
Whatever his existential stature.

Something we must simply accept,
To take the burden off the mind,
And in that act of acceptance.
Lasting peace happily find.

80.

Jealous Of My Time Is The World

Jealous of my time is the world, why?
My moments are sublimely mine,
Lost am I in the throes of ecstasy,
When in communion with the holy and divine.

For peace in the heart and mind is unmatched,
When I am to this world unattached,
No rivers dry and no trees bare,
No hovering clouds then hanging there.

No mist to hide the morning dew,
No sages needed, no sermons wise,
Cos my heart tells me what to do,
And do so too my seeing eyes.

The mind then all crystal clear,
No place for doubt, no room for fear,
As hand in hand I walk with Belief,
With radiance around, no trace of grief.

What more do you, O traveller, seek,
Your journey on earth not yours, to keep,
A stage and no more is this life for you,
Before it's time to bid it adieu.

81.
Commit To Happiness

Commit yourself to Happiness,
Then from yourself you won't divorced be,
And when the core within lies intact,
Nothing will ever cause misery.

Happiness then will cling to you,
As body does to soul,
And even when morose you feel,
You'll never feel less than whole.

The countenance that's happy,
Is your shield against the barb,
Of both Man and Destiny
When adverse is their garb.

The mind wants to be happy,
And so do all of us,
Why then do we ever choose,
To ride the 'unhappy' bus?

82.

Blurred Is The Line 'Tween Fact And Fiction

Blurred is the line 'tween fact and fiction,
When imagination takes soaring flight,
Things that we in the day don't see,
Reveal themselves in the dark of night.

Is fiction born from fact,
Or is the reverse of this true,
Did God create the Universe,
Or did Man create God too?

Must faith be beyond question,
Or is there place for some doubt,
Does doubt need an answer, I wonder,
Or must it be extinguished,
Put out?

Reality is finely nuanced,
The balance well-weighed,
The scales of justice not too uneven,
When the world you've carefully surveyed.

And when the final die is cast,
There is no going back,
So put today's troubles behind you,
And, thankfully, hit the sack.

83.

The River Of Life

Where the river leads to,
Is where my boat shall go,
For I neither know its future course,
Nor anything of its flow.

Life too is like the river,
Coursing through night and day,
O'er rock and crag, rough and smooth,
On its fickle way.

The journeys of both quite similar,
The river's quest the sea,
While life meanders through the years,
In search of eternity.

To merge, to meld, to one become,
That is but everyone's Destiny.

84.

The Fallacy Of Wisdom And Age

What use the wisdom that comes with age,
When frailty is the tolling bell,
The mind and spirit of the sage,
With nothing left to say or tell.

Leaves turn yellow as time goes by,
And the trees begin to pine,
For they know there is a time for all,
And that order is divine.

Nothing but nothing lives for ever,
Nor is anything so designed,
So wisdom at the end of the day,
Couldn't have been so divined.

Act wisely then whatever the age,
For even the wise act foolishly,
So whatever the number on your age's page,
Take heart from that and smilingly.

85.
The Mind Knows No Boundaries

The mind knows no boundaries
And dreams have no walls,
You can soar past the mountains
When the inner voice calls,

The sky is not the limit
And the earth doesn't confine,
Oceans are no barriers
To the one who can divine,

For the spirit within you
And your everlasting soul,
Can make that little 'You'
Much larger than whole.

You're part of the infinite
No less and no more,
Remember, through the journey called Life
You will, one day, reach the shore.

86.
Life vs Death

How quiet the environs of the cemetery,
How peaceful the world of the departed,
Why then do we fear the end so much?
Perhaps, death needs to be better marketed.

Let's call in the Ad guys shall we,
Let's decide on the budget and plan,
To prove to the gullible world of today,
Why living is futile, for both woman and man.

We'll tom-tom the virtues of permanent peace,
When peacefully you've breathed your last,
The present we decry and the future's unknown,
And the less said the better of the past.

Each one alive is at someone's throat,
Cloak and dagger the game,
Except for the few who 'think' they rule,
The rest don't even have a name.

O, how wonderfully classless is the world of the dead,
Where all are equal cos no one's there,
No name, no fame, no passports needed,
Buried or burnt, then God knows where.

Now isn't it clear beyond all shadow of doubt,
Haven't I proved my case?
My Lord, life needs to be thrown out,
When death stares, life's not even in the race.

Solicitors and Ad men of the world unite,
Write the Obit and all will be well,
Peace you will gain and so will mankind,
When the only sound left is the tolling bell.

Under the ground or up in flames,
Death beats Life any day,
Think about it, but carefully,
And you will smile at what I say.

87.

The Writing On The Wall

When the writing on the wall
Is what we fail to see,
That's when those with sight
Are indeed a mystery.

For nothing is more obvious
Than that which faces you,
Like reflections in the mirror,
Though not always true.

But, alas, not given to man
Is the definition of clarity?
Carried away, as he often is,
By glitz and imagery.

Keep your eyes and ears open
But the heart and mind too,
Misjudgements you will make,
But the errors will be few.

88.

Do I Like What The Mirror Shows Me?

Do I like what the mirror shows me,
Or am I with time displeased,
For the ravages caused to body and mind,
Am I unjustly aggrieved?

Or am I wise and accept,
The due processes of life,
Thus save myself head and heart ache,
Needless worry and strife?

When the choice of life wasn't mine,
And life I didn't select,
I must on this journey then, mustn't I,
Ponder and carefully reflect?.

The world's no more than a wayside inn,
To spend nights and days,
A sojourn it is till time is up,
Never mind what anyone says.

So next you see Time gone by,
In your looking-glass, my friend,
Some wrinkles and some silver hair,
And the spine begin to bend,
Think of the splendid times you've had,
And, on worry, no time should you spend.

89.

Sing Me A Song Of Hope And Joy

Sing me a song of hope and joy,
No plaintive melodies for me,
Dawn is what I'm waiting for,
And the rising rhapsody.

In the guise of the Orb in a colourful sky
Hope springs forth in my heart,
Eternal as the sun, it lives within,
And of me is an integral part.

Baleful would existence be
If hope and I weren't hand in hand,
With hope I bring joy to life,
Cos futile is the head in the sand.

With despair and fear and lurking doubt
Of moments that are yet to unfold,
What chance do I have without a sliver of Hope,
To triumph, to act bold.

So unlike clutching at straws in the wind,
I cling to both faith and hope,
They help me through the journey called Life,
And with inclement weather, cope.

90.

Sunlight And Shade

Does a bud ever ask the flower around,
What colour shall I be?
Or does the river its bed ever query,
Tell me the way to the sea?

Few things are ever prettier
Than a tall, standing tree,
But have you ever heard it whisper,
Come, come look at me.

And the tree as it wistfully ages,
Is laden with fruit aplenty,
For all to pick and joyfully so,
To lighten the load of the tree.

But this tree that does the shade provide,
Does inhibit the sunlight too,
Remember, Ashok, there's a time for all things,
And this will always, always hold true.

91.
O Death, Don't Arrogant Be

O Death, thou art no more than a sentinel,
On guard outside Life's door,
Knowing full well you too shall die
With me, and then be no more,
For you are to each one assigned
And so, you too must mortal be,
Servant and Master the two of you,
But who is who, tell me?

If longevity defines the relation
Then Life must clearly the winner be,
Cos you're never more than a moment's strike,
However peaceful or bitter, you see.

And when the flame of Life lies extinguished,
Darkness is what is spread,
Why must I then in fear tremble
Why must I live in dread,
Of you.

I've passed that door a million times
Where you in agony wait,
But never have I been in haste,
To call you in from the gate.

Cos the more I love Life I know
The greater is the wait you endure,
Suffering in silence and powerlessly,
As I romp with Life for sure.

I feel sorry for you O Death, I do,
You're just a word for the end of Life,
Aren't you?

92.
Fulfilment

A whole life spent and still a void,
An emptiness hard to fill,
Is fulfilment an eternal desire
That Man must suffer?
Until…

What is it that so afflicts him,
Why a restive, hankering soul,
Just being, doing nothing,
Is this even a thinkable goal?

Time's no river that passes us by,
So changing times it cannot be,
Is it writ for mankind to forever seek,
The handiwork of Destiny?

Is tranquillity a mirage?
A beating, thumping, heart the norm?
Is mortality a blessing
Or, a curse in another form?

How long is the tunnel, and at the end is there light?
Will there be sunrise, at the end of each night?

93.

Fandangle

'Tis in the nature of things, O Poet,
For heaven to remain where it is,
For were it to descend on earth,
Hell would go out of 'biz'.

Peace to the detriment of war,
Imagine this laughable scene,
No guns to glisten, no ships to build,
GDPs would plummet and only peacocks preen,

Turmoil and mayhem would foreign words be,
And rivers of nectar flow everywhere,
Johnny Walker Black would surely turn blue,
Wonder what Sammy, my friend, would do?

With 'houries' around, one per man,
For that is what the Lord ordains,
What would wives do I'd hate to think,
Where would they take their aches and pains?

So, why pray for heaven when hell's so good?
The devil known is always better.
Don't get me wrong you pious men,
Heaven's the spirit but hell the letter.

94.

Yes I'm Gullible

Yes, I'm gullible
And you can sell me for a song,
But manipulation is the synonym
Not for what is right, but the wrong.

Trust is never weak,
And faith is very strong,
And those that manipulate,
Don't last very long.

And nothing do I lose
If you sell me down the river,
Cos He not you is my guide,
And my Provider.

All those who carry a heart
Are soft and sincere no doubt,
But don't mistake that for weakness,
For they can be very stout.

95.

Celebrate The Life That's Fully Lived.

Celebrate the life that's fully lived,
No need for tears to be shed,
Reflect on the pages of Life's book,
And enjoy what you saw and read.

Memories are what stay behind,
And those we must always treasure,
To give peace to those who leave us,
And, to ourselves, in full measure.

The ephemeral nature of life is known,
And like buds that turn to flower,
Destiny's will reigns supreme,
Which for all, has writ the hour.

If the departed do but tears see,
They too will grieve in melancholy,
So smile whenever you think of them,
Cos everyone is, to someone, a beautiful gem.

96.

What Would Tranquillity Be Without Turmoil

What would tranquillity be without turmoil?
A placid sea without a storm,
A spring without a loaded coil,
An abstract thought without a form,

A bed of roses without soil,
Freedom without accompanying norm,
Reward without sweat and toil,
Transgression without reform,

Dawn without a rising sun,
Plus without a minus sign,
Celebration without joy and fun,
A focus just on thine and mine?

Nothing at all is the answer for me,
The natural state is best for all,
Cos futile would existence be,
If there was rise but no fall.

97.

O Death, Are You But Life In Another Form

O Death, are you but Life in another form,
Of which I but nothing know,
Paradise or purgatory,
Where willy-nilly, I shall go?

When I my heaven and hell make
On earth, with words and deeds my own,
What care have I for things extraneous,
With you why should I pick a bone?

The left hand knows not what the right does,
And so it is with Life and true,
Cos Life too is unaware,
Of when it will bow to you.

98.
Momentary Disenchantment

Is this tree lonely like me, I wonder,
Despite its ten thousand leaves and more,
Must I too a smiling happiness feign,
Even as the heart grieves, mightily sore?

Is the world about masks and men of straw,
And is nothing beyond the games they play?
Then what is reality and the substance of truth,
Do we really mean yes, when 'yes' we say?

Will things last beyond this night of sleep?
Will they ever be the same again?
Will I go beyond this breath of mine?
Or be free of tormenting pain?

Who knows what conundrums are,
For whoever lives beyond demise,
There is a world of stars on high,
And, the rest no other than a pack of lies.

Why must I darken my mood, Ashok,
So you, my friend, can then see the light,
The orange glow that paints the sky,
As sunrise bids the night goodbye.

99.

Tear Drops From Heaven And Cascading Falls

Tear drops from heaven and cascading falls,
The green of the mountains, the arid land galls,
The tumult of the seas, the thunder of the skies,
The wail of a starling and my heart cries,
Now seldom do I hear the nightingale sing,
Cos the breeze is so heavy no sounds does it bring,
No joy in the trees, no leaves do I see,
For barren today is my very own tree,
The snows are pretty but they do tie me down,
But I shan't let the gloom turn ugly and frown,
For spring can't be far
When winter I've endured,
And weather, like Time,
Changes,
I'm assured.

100.

Who Am I?

Am I that which I don't wish to be,
For there is a soul all charged within me,
That does but think and feel differently,
And therein lies the dichotomy,
Who Am I ?

The one I seem to be,
Or,
The one who is the real me,
And is this not just charade, make-believe,
Cos truth I don't wish to see,
For ugly it is that then faces me.
The Devil within that chides, but laughingly,

And Innocence,
The veiled beauty that hides shamefacedly,
For it knows no better,
Cos that is its nature true,
Majestic in its innocence.

101.
Befriend Yourself

Dark nights and days will come and go,
As the cycle of life unfolds,
Dawn, sunrise, sunset and night,
Is what the eye and the mind beholds.

One little star is all I need,
For my heart to come alight,
And however dark it may well be,
Resplendent is then my night.

For when the heart is brightly lit,
The mind and the eyes see better,
When heavy hangs the air within,
I'm chained in spirit and letter.

I'm free when I'm with myself,
Cos solitude is freedom,
To do what I wish and as I please,
Set my beat, walk with my drum.

No greater friend will you find,
Nor should you ever seek,
Than the one that resides within you,
With whom you seldom speak.

Befriend yourself and you will find,
How full your life can be,
When nothing else will you ever need,
Go try it and you will see.

102.
From A Full House

To the eerie quiet again,
I revert to the sounds of silence again,
The sparkle, the joy, the effervescence,
That walked out of the door
Returns, resounds,
To haunt.

The mind,
A product of involuntary thought and will,
Does me with a loneliness fill,
Which I discard in the time that it takes to me overwhelm,
Cos for me quiet is all when I am at the helm,
Of my life's ship.

And those moments of reflection and solitude,
I employ to dispel lingering doubt,
To within me spread calm,
For tranquillity is balsam and balm,
At least,
For me.

For if I can't my own best friend be,
How will I ever another trust?

103.
My Life, My World

I seek the folds of blessed night,
To sheath my tired eyes,
Tired from staying awake too long,
Tired of the day's lies.

A sun that does but hide the stars,
Is no great comfort for me,
A sky with starry gentle light,
Is what I wish to see.

So I can be in a world of my own,
Sleep, dream or lie awake,
And in the tangle that abounds,
My own Utopia make.

Where I can live on the terms I want,
Without the liable 'naiveté',
Without approvals of those around,
That I now need to get.

Dreams are but dreams, Ashok,
Escapism is what the wise call it,
Two hoots to such wisdom friends,
When my heart it is that's lit.

Never stepping on toes not mine,
Pray tell me what crime I commit,
My life, my world, and I'm entitled,
As I wish to simply live it.

104.

Rambling

Do you know the river that never dries,
The grieving heart that never cries,
The tears that never leave the eyes,
And the sadness hidden in the skies?

Bright as stars seemingly are,
All things look pretty from afar,
Proximity tends to often mar,
A close encounter could be a smashed car.

Not all trees are always green,
Peacocks don't always preen,
Not all folks say what they mean,
And what, tell me, is a perennial scene?

For nothing was ever designed to last,
Not even a shady past,
The pace of change threateningly fast,
Nothing was ever in stone cast.

Rambling does de-clutter the mind,
Welcome the emptying, after a grind,
Things you lose are good to find,
And nights are meant to just unwind.

Before you then say good night,
Before you turn off the light,
Before you go out of sight,
Before you start another fight,
Ramble please, with all your might.

105.

Wayward Is The Mind

Can this the turning day be,
For points are but too small,
To make a vow and keep it,
And not make promises tall?

Wander does the mind always,
Tempered by desire,
Asleep does poor Conscience lie,
Till prodded by conditions dire.

Do we a bit of the hammer need,
To do what we should always do,
And not get lost in pious intent,
Then forget, repent and rue?

How woefully weak the human flesh,
Weaker still the mind,
Toughen it up and realize,
You can easily the strength find.

Wayward romps my wayward mind,
Aware but not afraid,
Of lurking dangers and shadows grey,
When inept choices are made.

106.

Saints and Sinners

Why do I so inadequate feel,
Then cower before the image I face?
For are we not all deeply flawed?
Saints and sinners both, in Life's race?

Show me the saint who has not sinned,
And I'll show you the saint in every sinner,
All races remember end one way,
In every loser there lives a winner.

Without trespass would we redemption need,
And with whom does the power of forgiveness lie?
If divine is that right does it not say,
All who tread the earth must look up to the sky?

Sainthood is conferred by no other than Man
On those he considers 'mostly' good,
The key word here is mostly, friends,
And that must be rightly understood.

For good we're all in the main.
So cast not stones, refrain.

107.

The Convulsions Of Climate

O Man you'll pay and dearly so,
For the convulsions you put climate through,
The change is subtle but real for sure,
And climate will only blame you.

The way you live and with it play,
Is plain for all to see,
Your unquenchable thirst for material progress,
Will, sadly, alter your destiny.

Plants that help you breathe and live,
Are the ones you destroy with no care,
When you're done with all forests deep,
At arid land you'll stare.

With emissions of all kinds and more,
And billowing smoke in the skies,
You may soon be looking at starless nights,
With your very own hapless eyes.

Voices in the wilderness,
Are voices nonetheless,
Nature will its lessons teach,
If you don't deal with your mess.

Harken to the voices sane,
That simplicity propound,
Nature is your friend, not bane,
Your need for it is profound.

So befriend it, heed it and happy you shall be,
Ignore it and devastation will be your destiny.

108.
A Good Man

No mind is greater than another mind,
And to charity I'm not inclined,
No mind is inferior to another either,
And we all succumb to rigor.

Worthless is he who worthless thinks
For no one here's without some kinks,
Kings and Queens and Presidents too,
Fall from grace, like me and you.

Cos the fallen angel resides within,
Embodying greed, ambition and sin,
Saint is he who saintly lives,
And of his time and self, freely gives.

When you look at the mirror, what should you see,
Cos a good man is all you need to be,
Anything else is just a loss,
Cos the mirror will then be your daily boss.

109.
Life's Like The Bud

From bud to flower is an age gone by,
As one blooms the other takes a bow,
Time and Life do quickly fly,
Enjoy each moment of the here and now.

Spring arrives and brings the buds,
As winter shifts its abode elsewhere
The buds look sweet but in waiting mode,
As flowers begin to bloom out there.

Each bud grew by the hour,
Enjoyed the care and gaze bestowed
By those who came to savour spring,
And joy share as the morning glowed.

The buds danced and swayed too
In the gentle breeze that often blew,
Knowing their joy could ephemeral be,
Their fate in the hands of whom,
They knew.

For the one to bloom the other must die,
Cos bud to flower is the journey of life.
Have you ever seen a bud that's sad?
Have you ever seen a bud in strife?

So live life smiling as the bud does,
Cos the story's the same for man too,
Why fear anything with a God above?
You decide if what I say is true.

110.

He Cools Me Down

He cools me down when it's hot out here,
He with the fan above,
No walls, no ceilings does He need,
His mercies, He showers with love.

The breeze that descends from the heavens above,
Pure balm for the sweat of my brow,
It lightens my being and frees the soul,
Bringing smiles to my face, and how.

Then look up I do at the skies all blue,
The sun, the stars, and thc moon,
By day and by night as time goes by,
There's spring in my step and very soon,
I'm thankful for His blessing and boon.

111.
Empowerment

With empowerment and equality,
Women feel divine,
But go ask Indra Nooyi
And she'll tell you, it ain't all fine.

There are two sides to every story,
And every coin that you see,
There's a feel-good factor to empowerment,
And a certain negativity.

What or who is right on this
Is for each one to decide,
In a world where freedom in any form,
Is just taken for a ride.

Happiness must the determinant be,
The final arbiter the Self,
And while independence has a point to make,
Happiness is neither power nor pelf.

Life is a game of percentages
A little less or more,
If your scale weighs in for happiness,
You've made right choices for sure.

112.

What Are We?

A strange amalgam of youth and age,
Of decadence and morality are we,
God and Satan both within us,
Why is this, tell me?

Racked 'tween pillar and the proverbial post,
The mind torn asunder,
The devil within to the god inside
Does, but revoltingly, surrender.

Alas, we are thus designed,
By the one we look up to,
Then who amongst us can a stone cast,
For tainted we all are, isn't that true?

Imperfect is the Universe
And so an imperfect Man,
Do what he will or what he desires,
There are limits to what he can.

Accept yourself and happily then,
Built as you naturally are,
Before you do attempts make,
To tarnish and another's image mar.

113.

See Through The Maze

A silent heart, a quiet mind,
O where, will I such tranquillity find
In the hurly-burly of the world today
Where words have but little to say?

What help can I of the trees ask,
When survival for them is itself a task?
Will stars that shine up on high,
Come to my aid and what of the sky?

And what of night,
That keeper of dreams,
Will I dream of streams and swimming breams,
Or will sharks lie in wait for me,
And sleep turn alien entity?

Wrong conclusions have you drawn,
From the jungle, your home of old,
For you've turned the world all upside down,
You need, O Man, to be clearly told.

Frenetic pace and unbridled action,
Your desire to inhabit the stars,
What is your problem with home,
The Earth,
That you have to go looking for Mars?

A restful mind and a peaceful heart
Don't go with greed and lust,
The dollar's taken the smile off your face,
Just look at your 'Upper Crust'.

Accept, if you will, that the purpose of life
Is only to happy be,
Then you will see the light of day,
In no more than half a jiffy.

114.

The Centuries Old Race

When 80's on the horizon in a 100 yard race,
Reality is tough to evenly embrace,
For the candle of hope begins melting away
And a flicker is all that then lights the way.

Looking over the shoulder does a pastime become,
At the distance you've covered and you might turn glum
As you recount the years and the decades gone by,
And, with feet on the ground, you look up at the sky.

Wistfully imploring the heavens, as it were,
To reveal the morrow, however blur,
And think of the sun's imminent demise,
With hope in the heart of another sunrise.

What remarkable things does aging do,
Crease the forehead and wrinkle it too,
Knocks teeth out of the biting equation,
Makes it difficult to spell the word 'elation'.

Ah! but there's still 20 to go,
For the river to merge with the sea,
But who wants to go o'er rock and crag,
But I can speak only for me.

115.
Bondage

Free me from oppression, O Lord,
Of both Man and the Soul,
These faithful allies known for long,
Have alas left me less than whole.

To this land and air and the water too,
Have I accustomed become,
For it is from them that I earned my peace of mind,
And not to this world succumb.

A wonderful journey it has been,
And like a magnificent, turbulent sea,
Mostly calm and vastly regal,
Not often a stormy entity,

But unshackled freedom remains the goal,
Of all who tread the earth,
Salvation, the eternal wish,
From the time that Man took birth.

Bondage even to the self is but misery, Ashok,
Let these words sink into you, let them deeply soak.

116.
The Survivor

He smiled his way through rough and smooth
And like the river gently flowed,
Resilience was his chosen watchword,
And in ample measure it showed.

He walked the gardens of palaces,
And trudged on lonely lands,
Played with dawn and the rising sun,
And in swirling, hostile, sands.

Snows he plucked off mountains,
And the depths of misery measured,
But every moment of his life
He smilingly, treasured.

For he knew, understood and accepted,
The veracity of night and day,
And did what he thought he had to,
Unmindful of what people say.

They called him the great survivor,
The one who never gave up,
The one who knew cuisine,
And the travails of an empty cup.

He had a name for sure, like all
But they called him, the Survivor.

117.
Did You Know?

Did you know?
Those that with the river flow,
Never Drown.

Those with smiles on their faces,
Even when they lose their races,
Rarely Frown.

Those that awake early morn,
Fresh as daisies at crack of dawn,
Are always Up, never Down.

And no one's happier than,
Either woman or any man,
Than the one who plays the merry Clown.

Goodness needs no wrappers,
Neither tatters
Nor, Resplendent Gown.

And care means nothing more than love,
No golden robes, no velvet glove,
No Eiderdown.

And no wearier head was ever there,
Nor greater burdens ever share,
Than the one that wears a thorny Crown.

118.
Harmony

I am not even a dot in my little world,
Yet how grandly I speak of the Universe,
One little tree is bigger than me,
And that's not just a line from some verse.

A hillock I find tough to climb,
And the Arctic gives me the freeze,
I shudder to think of tsunamis,
When flattened I am by the breeze.

Grandiose, the plans that I make,
As is the will to conquer all,
Nature, the stars and the moon,
Blissfully unaware of my fall.

When harmony, not conquest, should the mantra be,
With the rest that also exist,
Dependent as we are on each other,
Why do we, each other, resist?

Imagine, if stars were to emit no light,
Even though it may only be reflected,
Our journeys on earth would be
Only rough and obstructed.

Decimation of Nature and the species,
Disregard of biodiversity,
No bigger challenge confronts,
No bigger calamity.

It's still not too late, O Man,
To redeem yourself for your sake,
But it will cruelly and surely,
More than pious intent, take.

119.
Technology - Boon or Bane?

I can call a million miles,
And instantly connect,
For business or for pleasure,
I can now call direct.

And it costs me next to nothing
To now communicate,
Via email and the 'apps',
I can all desires sate.

I can move both heaven and earth
With the simple click of a mouse,
And would you believe it
Without even leaving my house.

Humans are untrustworthy,
So with robots I feel safer,
Canines are my favourite
But I could even do with a heifer.

From one end to the other,
Is now a matter of hours,
Celebrations now don't need people,
You can do it with just flowers.

You can Google your way through life
And the GPS will get you there,
But what will you do, pray tell me
If the host has no time to spare?

Could we do all this and more
Without the aid of technology?
Impossible we would say,
Supremely confident but unhappy,

For we have given the reins to another,
It's called the 'monster' machine,
It's given us physical comfort,
But made living less serene.

We used to live shorter lives,
But relatively problem free,
A hundred and more is nearly par,
But only with docs and surgery.

What used to take an eternity?
Was the ship that endlessly sailed?
But whoever in the good old days,
Against serene waters, ever railed.

Technology is surely a boon,
But not if a Frankenstein we create,
The Master must always Man be,
And help fulfil his fate.

120.
Poison Kills Poison

Toxins that I myself create,
Pride, greed, delusion, hate,
Gnaw inside and take their toll,
Leave me racked and less than whole.

Silent killers are these all,
Power, pelf and lust enthral,
But a price we pay for everything,
Excessive joy does tears bring.

Poison kills poison is an adage old,
Among the stories that granny told,
So,
The antidote is to bear in mind,
And yourself often remind,
The frame in which you ensconced are,
Is far from eternal, very far.

121.

The Child Within

As the plant does the seed carry within,
So does Man the child too,
But while the plant does not the seed forget,
Of Man that is not always true.

The disconnect does its toll take,
In the form of the arrogant man,
For whoever does the roots forget,
Will never be stable, nor can.

A rootless tree will no shade provide,
No comfort from the heat,
No warmth deliver in the winter's chill,
Staying alive itself, a great feat.

And so it is with the one who does
The child within forget,
Who is happier, dear reader, tell me,
Than the one who has that child met?

What more do we want than peace of mind,
And a little bit of joy,
The innocent smile of that child left behind,
Whether with doll or another toy.

So stay in touch with that child within you,
And that connect you will, but, never rue.

122.
Let's Treat The Past

Let's treat the past with warmth and care,
For with every single passing day,
A step nearer the end we are,
And the past is the friend on the way.

To help us through the future walk,
And mistakes not repeat,
And like the mirror that tells you constantly,
When you look dead beat.

But live in the past we must not,
For the future then will be bleak,
Flounder we will and waywardly,
In the maze of the past, so to speak.

Visit and engage sometimes,
The past we should see as a friend,
And no more than the occasional glance and ear,
Should we to it lend.

123.

The Love For Words

That passion's gone,
Like love that flies out of the window, forlorn,
Like a child that arrives, stillborn,
Too much of anything, even love or goodness,
Dulls over time.
For after all,
Nothing, not even life, is ever eternal,
So why should one element of it be any different,
Days and nights too alternate, don't they?
Does any sea ever guarantee
That it will be forever calm?
Or a prayer that ensures freedom from harm?

No bud assures it will turn to flower,
Nor Time that you will get another hour,
Nor the heaviness in the air that it will lift,
Nor clouds vanish to give you the sun as a gift.
Then,
Why should the love for words last?
Or will it like the homing bird
The message deliver and return?
Who knows the answers ever?

124.
Promise Myself

I vow to myself to cheerful be,
And not let moods over-take me,
But the sun I see struggle too,
When skies are dark not azure blue.

And thus do I console the mind,
And some cheer within strive to find,
Beyond the horizon, hopefully, peer,
And of the morrow myself remind,

Fall back on some old memory
Of mountains climbed and conquered seas,
Of starlit nights and festival's lights,
Of romance and the fragrant breeze.

And then as I close my eyes,
With a prayer on the lips and a look at the skies,
I hope it's dreams that I see,
An anguished heart, soulfully, cries.

O, for the innocence of the child,
A dimpled smile and manner mild,
Childhood was another world,
From the call of the jungle and the modern wild

125.
Hello, My Beating Heart

Hello tick tock, tick tock,
Who has the key to this damn clock?
The one that only once but stops,
And when it does, it irretrievably drops

The one who its owner is,
The one, who because of it lives,
Its sound no more than rhythmic beats,
Such melody was only known to Keats,

But fidelity was not its forte ever,
It's known to ties suddenly sever,
Why then am I its humble slave,
Cos my life, dear friends, I wish to save.

Long live then my beating heart
I know I haven't looked after you,
Nor played well my given part,
But can I reparations make?
And can we not make another start?
Please forgive me
O, Dear Heart.

126.

Whispers

The sounds of the running brook,
The rustle of those leaves,
The whispers that I, O forsook,
When I chose these regal eaves.

The romance of the countryside,
The swaying daffodils,
Whispers always by my side,
And those swinging windmills.

Those flapping wings, those coloured birds,
Flying to and fro,
The whispers of unspoken words,
They never seem to go.

I miss those whispers and a lot
The green of the forest glade,
And often wonder what I've got,
From all the riches that I have made.

127.
Life

Don't tell me what love is,
Don't tell me what life is,
Between living and dying
Don't tell me what strife is.

And it's all in the mind,
The games that we play.
With just one road to follow,
We still lose our way.

We climb all the mountains,
And plumb all the seas,
Then get blown away,
By the gentlest of breeze.

There is an angel within us,
That resides in us all,
And a devil that schemes
To bring about the fall.

The gusts of ego,
The winds of vanity,
Ephemeral they are,
And fragile is serenity.

Every moment serene
Is no less than eternity,
Every moment encompasses,
Life in totality.

128.
Time Is A Constant - Only Man Changes

"Time makes ancient good uncouth",
O, how far removed that is from truth,
For goodness does but never alter,
However much that Man may falter.

Commandments have stood the test of time,
Writ in stone, tablet or hymns and rhyme,
Life and death no different now,
You get to heaven the same old how.

And if hell is where you will reside,
It's cos you were uncouth inside,
And untruth now was falsehood then,
Nothing changes with a golden pen.

Mores may change but values don't,
Right from wrong mustn't and won't,
'Modern' doesn't make all things right,
Of things ancient, we mustn't lose sight.

The present will one day the past be,
And that is the future of both you and me,
De-link yourself from your past,
And you will soon be extinct and fast.

Robot, O Man, you are not,
Nor is that your destined lot,
The pursuit of progress, mindlessly,
Will neither reveal nor alter your destiny?

Never decry the ancient times,
Never forget old nursery rhymes,
Never forget the one above,
Man's bonding is nothing but love.

Quote from American poet
James Russell Lowell, 1845

129.
Seasons

Another summer wends its way
Into autumnal arms,
Balmy breeze and drops of rain,
Colours bright and swaying palms.

And I begin to winter dread,
The thought of cold does the bones chill,
Deriving comfort now instead,
From the heat that summer does instil,

The colours of autumn enchanting indeed,
Red, green, orange and gold,
For an eternal autumn do I plead,
My heart for ever sold.

Eternal is just mirage,
Inspired by fear and some hope,
Envisage not 'for ever' and
You will, with life, then nicely cope.

130.
Wisdom

When the eyes reveal more than words,
Why not then silence embrace,
For through the follies of the tongue,
Why run yourself out of the race?

Wisdom needs no verbal expression,
For it lies at the very core,
Contemplation is all it needs,
And it never asks for anything more.

Listen is what it always asks,
For words are prone to many plays,
Wisdom rarely needs to wisdom speak,
Through revolving nights and days.

Wise is he who engages with
A Conscience that's alert,
For neither he nor anyone else,
Does then, in life get hurt.

So weigh your thoughts a million times,
Before they turn to speech,
The fountainhead of wisdom lies,
Within everyone's easy reach.

Haikus

1. *Cherries and blossoms,*
   Herald the advent of Spring,
   As Nature smiles wordlessly.

2. *The blue from the sky,*
   Lends its colour to the sea,
   How close heaven and earth.

3. *Prayer, the most powerful*
   Antidote to bouts of pain,
   Like dewdrops, like rain.

4. *Bananas the fruit*
   That can drive you all crazy
   Don't go bananas.

5. *Snows melt to rivers form*
   That twist and turn endlessly
   In search of eternity.

6. *Think, touch , hear, see, smell,*
   Those that only with eyes see,
   Miss the world's beauty.

7. *Winds change direction*
   Treasure the moments of joy
   You never know when.

8. *You are your best friend*
   Be alone but not aloof,
   Solitude is peace.

9. *An eagle in flight*
Soaring over distant clouds,
What a glorious sight.

10. *Much like rivulets*
Tears are meant to flow and dry
The cycle goes on.

11. *Some puzzles aren't solved*
The world is a conundrum
Life is mystery.

12. *I gaze at the stars*
As the moon shines down on me
The night is heavenly.

13. *I heard a bird sing*
The voice was heavenly
Was it an angel?

14. *The tree gives us shade*
Why don't we treat it kindly
I wonder sometimes?

15. *Tigers and rhinos*
Live together happily
Then why shouldn't Man?

16. *A beautiful smile*
Like a beautiful flower
Always nice to see.

17. *Secrets that you keep*
Well concealed within your heart
The eyes will reveal.

18. *Sweep cobwebs away*
Cos they will clutter the mind
And then entrap you.

19. *Nights are meant for sleep*
And dreams, to keep hopes alive
Castles in the air.

20. *Tranquillity lies*
In the shrines within the heart
Not in stone temples.

21. *Green leaves, Brown leaves all,*
Oak trees, Elm trees, Fir trees all
Nature is supreme.

22. *I wish I could fly*
Somewhere miles into the sky
Soar and dream and soar.

23. *Don't ask the gardener*
Which flower is the prettiest
No mother will choose.

24. *Deep down in the heart*
Every adult is a child
Every tree a seed.

25. *Storms know and winds too*
You can bend a reed but, then
The reed will stand tall.

Quatrains

1. *Happiness is a piece of cake,*
A slice or two is yours to take,
But there's other fish in the pond too,
So you must indeed share it, for God's sake.

2. *You must with yourself some time spend,*
Only then will you learn, my dear friend,
Something of this complexity called Life,
That from the beginning carries the inevitable end.

3. *Don't ever try your sorrows to drown,*
Hangovers will leave you with more than a frown,
Sceptre and mace, signs of grace,
But uneasy the head that wears the crown.

4. *Ephemeral indeed is pleasure pure,*
Not designed to ever last,
Why then do you to it succumb
Are we just actors in a cast?

5. *Patience will be rewarded, always,*
Effort will be lauded, always,
If sincerity is your middle name,
Your speech will be applauded, always.

6. *How beautiful the cooing of the dove is,*
How pure and uplifting the sky above is,
You can gaze at the stars and the moon if you wish,
But the eyes alone tell you what true love is.

7. *How far have I come I wish to know,*
But who will tell me when I've walked alone,
There's a price to be paid for transgressions all,
And for these willy-nilly all must atone.

ND - #0248 - 080726 - C0 - 197/132/14 - PB - 9781784560935 - Gloss Lamination